Guaranteed Success for Grade School

50 Easy Things You Can Do Today!

Marrae Kimball

Original Edition

Find Your Way Publishing, Inc.
PO BOX 667
Norway, Maine

Guaranteed Success for Grade School
50 Easy Things You Can Do Today!
By Marrae Kimball

ISBN-13: 978-0-9824692-3-1
ISBN-10: 0-9824692-3-3

Find Your Way Publishing, Inc.
PO BOX 667
Norway, ME 04268 U.S.A.

Orders at www.FindYourWayPublishing.com

First Edition, 2010

Printed in the United States of America.

This book is dedicated to all of my family and friends with love. To all the children in grade school learning to become better people, and to all the teachers who are teaching us!

And last but not least, to all of the men and women who serve in the military and fight for our freedom, this includes the 251st Sapper Company of the Maine Army National Guard, my uncle Scott Bowen, and my dad, Curtis William Kimball Jr.

Thank you!!!

Acknowledgments

I would like to thank God for giving me strength and for always being there with me. I'd like to thank everyone who supported me and helped me with this book. Thank you for all your suggestions and ideas. Special thanks to Reed Dyer and Cathy Emerson. To Kimberly Martin for the formatting and cover design. To my grandparents and siblings who gave me their advice. To my mom, Melissa for helping me with the typing and paper-work. Thank you every one!

"We can do anything that we want to do if we stick to it long enough."

Helen Keller

This book is given to you to help you learn 50 easy skills that you should know during grade school.

You will have fun practicing these simple steps.

You can do it!

And even if you already know these 50 things, you can still use this book as a reminder. Have fun, follow these simple steps, and remember that your teacher, parents, and friends will forever thank you for it!!!

Table of Contents

Table of Contents

Table of Contents

Guaranteed Success for Grade School

50 Easy Things You Can Do Today!

1

Good Morning!

Greet others by saying "Good morning" or "Hello" with a smile on your face. Try it! Say "Good morning" while smiling. It sounds so nice. You will always sound cheerful if you are smiling while greeting someone. To make it extra nice, say the person's name after the greeting. Say, "Good morning Ms. Edwards!" or "Hi Bailey!"

Greet teachers and other students with a smiling "Good morning" or "Hello" tomorrow and every day.

2

Say "Please" and "Thank you"

Get in the habit of always saying "please" and "thank you." Good manners are a habit and are very easy to learn. Practice saying "please" every time you ask for something from someone.

Can I please have a piece of paper?

Can I please sharpen my pencil?

Can I please play with you at recess? And also practice saying "thank you" every time someone does something nice for you.

Thank you for the piece of paper.

Thank you for letting me sharpen my pencil.

Thank you for playing with me at recess.

Always say please and thank you.

3

Line up nicely

Be nice while lining up. Lining up is not a race so do not push or cut. Think about it. If you push or cut in line you really are not going to get to where you are going that much faster.

If your class is lining up to go to the library and you cut in front of someone, you are only going to get to the library one second sooner and that will not make any difference at all. Even if you are last in line you will still get where you are going with the rest of your class.

If another student acts like they are in a hurry and they want to cut in line, surprise them by letting them. You know it won't make that much of a difference and you will make someone happy by letting him or her get in front of you.

Be nice while lining up.

4

Do not run inside

I know the hallways are big and long, but remember that once you step inside your school that your legs need to slow down.

If you run in school, you could easily fall and get hurt or cause someone else to fall and get hurt.

School is for learning and learning takes time. Take your time by walking.

Always walk in school.

5

Hats off

It is polite to take off your hat when you are inside a building and when you sit down to eat a meal.

If you go on a field trip and you wear a hat, just take it off as soon as you walk into a building. If you don't want to hold it, you can put it in your pocket. If it's a baseball cap you can unsnap it and hook it onto a belt loop on your pants.

If you are eating and you sit down to eat, take your hat off and place it on your knee or hang it on your chair.

It is a sign of respect to take your hat off while inside and while sitting down to eat.

6

Hang up your coat

Neatly hang up your coat after coming inside. If it falls down, pick it up.

If you have winter boots, hats, or mittens put them neatly where they go. Other students do not want to be tripping over your mess. And you don't want people walking on your things because who knows what is on the bottom of their shoes!

Always hang your coat up and put your boots, hats, and mittens neatly away.

7

Open doors for others

It is nice to hold the door open for others. Some school doors are really heavy and hard to open, especially for the kindergartners and first graders.

If you notice that someone is having a hard time opening a door or that they have their hands full with books or papers, always offer to help them by opening the door for them.

If you can, offer to open or hold the door for others.

8

Write your name
on your paper

Try to get in the habit of writing your name on your paper as soon as your teacher hands it out to you. This will help you get credit for your work and your teacher won't have to try to guess which student forgot to write their name.

As soon as you get a paper, write your name on it.

9

Raise your hand

When you are in class, be sure to raise your hand when you want to talk.

You can practice this at home if you want and have fun with it. Every time you want to say something, raise your hand first. Practicing at home can help you remember to do it when you are in the classroom.

This might be one of the most important lessons. If you want to say something or have a question, raise your hand and wait for your teacher to call on you. A teacher cannot teach if other students are talking when they are not supposed to be.

Remember to raise your hand when you want to say something.

10

Use your
big girl/big boy voice

Always talk in your big girl or your big boy voice. Please do not whine. Do you like to hear people using a whiny voice? No, because it can be annoying and unpleasant.

Always talk in a nice voice and if you catch yourself whining, just stop yourself and start using your regular voice. It will feel good and your friends and teachers will thank you.

Talk without whining.

11

Listen to your teacher

Be sure to have your listening ears on when your teacher is talking.

If your teacher tells you that it's time for math, sit up straight and pay attention.

If your teacher tells you that it's time to line up for lunch, quietly line up for lunch. It's really easy. Just listen!

Listen so you can do what your teacher tells you.

12

Good sportsmanship

You will play a lot of games in grade school. Games are for fun. Sometimes it can be upsetting to lose a game but always try to be a good-sport even if you lose a game. If someone else wins, be happy for them and say "Good job" because next time you might win. Try not to get grumpy or mad. Have you ever played a game and won and had the other person get mad at you? You don't want to do that to someone else.

The whole point of game playing is to have fun. When someone wins a game they deserve to be happy about it without being made to feel bad.

When playing games, be a good-sport.

13

Use your inside voice

School can be exciting and fun but please don't shout. Use your inside voice while inside and your outside voice while outside. It's really easy.

An inside voice is softer and quieter than an outside voice. When you are inside, the sound of your voice can bounce off the walls and interrupt or bother other students. When you are outside there are no walls, therefore, you can talk louder.

While inside your school building or any building, use your inside voice.

14

Be polite

Always be polite. There is no need to be rude or to talk rudely to someone. Nothing good can come from being rude. It's only going to cause you to be in a bad mood and to hurt someone's feelings.

If you catch yourself talking rude you can turn the situation around just as quickly by saying you're sorry and changing how you are talking. You are the one who decides how you are going to talk to others.

Always be kind and polite while talking to others.

15

Wait patiently

Sometimes we have so many good ideas and things on our minds that we want to blurt all of our thoughts out as we think of them but do not interrupt others.

Say, "Excuse me" if you want to join in a conversation when someone else is talking.

When you are in class, always raise your hand if you want to share your thoughts.

Do not interrupt. Instead wait patiently and say, "excuse me" or raise your hand.

16

Follow the
playground rules

While on the playground, have fun but follow the rules. Your teachers will explain the playground rules for you.

One rule at my school is no walking up the slides. Of course this is because if someone is sliding down the slide, the person walking up it would get hurt.

Rules are made for your safety. Follow them. You're a big kid now! You can do it!

Follow the rules on the playground.

17

Keep your
hands to yourself

This is an easy one. If it's not your body, then don't touch it. Don't poke, push or grab another student. Keep your hands to yourself.

If it's not your desk, don't get into it or touch something left on top of it.

If it doesn't belong to you, then don't touch it without permission.

Always keep your hands to yourself.

18

Do not tattle

Try not to snitch or tattle on other students. This can be a hard one to understand. I try to remember it this way, if someone gets hurt then you should tell a teacher. But if someone cuts in line or picks their nose, you don't need to tell your teacher.

Your teacher doesn't have time to listen to tattling all day. If you want to tell on someone just to get him or her in trouble, usually that is tattling. But if you are telling on someone who is hurting someone else or who is hurt, then that is not tattling.

Do not tattle.

19

Pledge of Allegiance

Always say the *Pledge of Allegiance* loud and proud. The *Pledge of Allegiance* is a promise to be loyal, true, and good citizens. The flag stands for the United States of America.

For me, it's also a sign of respect towards all the servicemen and women who have fought and risked their lives for our freedom.

When you say the *Pledge of Allegiance* and promise to be a good citizen, mean it and say it with pride.

20

Say "Excuse me"

It is polite to say, "Excuse me" after you sneeze, burp, cough, or let one rip (or as my mom calls it, pass gas). Although these are all natural things and happen to all of us, we need to say, "Excuse me" when it does.

Sneezing can be loud and any loud noise that seems to interrupt the class requires you to acknowledge it by using your manners.

Get in the habit of saying, "Excuse me" when needed.

21

Bless you

If someone sneezes, it is polite to acknowledge it by saying, "Bless you."

Achoo = Bless you.

22

Cough or sneeze into your elbow

Turn away from people when coughing or sneezing and always cough or sneeze into your elbow.

You don't want to sneeze or cough into your hands because you use your hands to touch so many things. That is how colds are spread to others.

When coughing or sneezing, cough or sneeze into your elbow.

23

Sit up straight

You should sit up straight in class and while eating lunch. Sitting up straight and tall in class not only shows your teacher that you are paying attention but it's good for your posture as well. Slouching can cause your back and shoulders to ache.

And sitting up straight while you eat your lunch helps your food digest better.

Always sit up straight and tall.

24

Pick up during lunch and snack time

While eating your snack if you spill your drink, get a napkin and wipe it up.

If some of your lunch falls on the floor, pick it up and throw it away.

Your cafeteria is clean when you first enter it because someone has worked very hard at cleaning it.

Make sure when you are done eating that your area is as clean as it was when you came in.

Pick up any food that you drop or spill while eating your snack or lunch.

25

Eat slowly

Eat slowly and don't shove food in your mouth.

Always chew your food with your mouth closed and don't talk while eating.

If you talk or chew your food with your mouth open, people can see your food all chewed up and not only does it look gross but it's not polite.

Eat slowly and chew with your mouth closed.

26

Always tell the truth

Sometimes it may seem easier to lie but if you don't tell the truth it will get you into bigger trouble. Sometimes it takes bravery to tell the truth but that is what becoming a big kid means.

Telling the truth is very important and your body knows right from wrong. Just like fruits and vegetables are good for your body, so is telling the truth!

Be brave and always tell the truth.

27

Eye Contact

When someone is talking to you, be sure to look him or her in the eye. Do not get distracted by things going on around you.

Making eye contact with the person you are talking with shows them that you are listening to them.

While talking to someone, always look him or her in the eyes.

28

Say you're sorry

If you make a mistake, say you're sorry. Everyone makes mistakes. Making mistakes can help us learn not to do it again. Saying sorry can be hard but is a sign of bravery.

If you make a mistake, be brave and say you're sorry.

29

Always
follow directions

This is really easy. Just do what your teacher asks you to do. It's your teacher's job to teach you, and it's your job as a student to follow directions. If you're not sure what to do, just raise your hand and ask.

Follow directions by doing as your teacher asks.

30

Push in your chair

Whenever you leave your desk, push your chair in. Not only will this make your area look neater but also, other students do not want to trip over the legs of your chair while walking by.

When leaving your desk, push your chair in.

31

Take compliments

When someone says something nice to you, say thank-you without putting yourself down.

It can sometimes make you feel uncomfortable when someone compliments you or says something nice about you, but resist the urge to say something negative about yourself.

If someone tells you that they like your jacket, don't say "Oh, this old thing", instead smile and say "thank you."

Always say thank-you when others compliment you.

32

Clean up after yourself

If something falls off or out of your desk don't ignore it or step over it, instead pick it up and put it away. It only takes a second to pick something up. When things are on the floor, not only can they get stepped on and break but it makes your area look like a mess.

If you see something on the floor, pick it up and put it away.

33

Give your
full attention

Always give your attention and look at the teacher or whoever is speaking or talking.

It is polite to look at your teacher while she is standing in front of the class and talking.

It is also important to look at a classmate giving a presentation. How would you feel if you were standing in front of the class talking about something important and other students were not paying attention to you? Your feelings would be hurt because it's not polite.

Always give your full attention and look at the person who is speaking at the front of the classroom.

34

No name calling
or bullying

Have you ever heard the saying, "If you don't have anything nice to say, don't say anything at all"? I try to remember this often.

Mean things that we say or do really hurt people. One of my mom's friends told me that when she was younger some of her friends asked if she was waiting for a flood because her pants were getting too short for her. Even though 20 years have gone by, she still checks to be sure her pants aren't too short before she leaves her house. Another person I know was told she had big ears as a child, since then she hardly ever wears her hair up.

Be careful what you say. Never be a bully or call others bad names.

35

National Anthem

The National Anthem is a song that stands for and honors our nation. The National Anthem is played before sports games and before other public events. Always stand up straight, put your right hand on your heart, take off your hat if you are wearing one, and do not talk during the entire song. If you are chewing gum, stop chewing while the song is playing.

Always be respectful when the National Anthem is playing.

36

Say "No thank-you"

You now know that you should always say please and thank-you but you should also say "no thank-you".

If someone offers you a pencil and you already have one, instead of saying "No, I don't need it, say, "No thank-you, I don't need it".

It is nice to say "No thank-you" because you are thanking the person for offering you something even though you don't need it or don't want it.

Say "No thank-you" when someone offers you something that you don't want or need.

37

Help your school

You can help your school in a lot of ways. A couple ways to help your school is by not wasting paper, napkins, paper-towels, etc.

Keep school supplies in good shape by treating them with care.

Some schools collect labels from certain food products that they can send in and exchange for money or school supplies.

School supplies are very expensive and you should do everything you can do to help your school.

38

Let others exit first

You know that you should open and hold the door for others. But did you know that when you are entering a classroom or building, an elevator or taxi, that you should always let the person exiting, exit first?

If you are walking into your classroom and another student is walking out at the same time, you should stop and let them exit first.

It is polite to let others exit before you enter.

39

Willingly do what your teacher asks

When your teacher asks you to do something, do it without complaining. Put a happy face on and say, "Okay, I will do it and I will do my best!" Remember how lucky you are to be able to learn.

Our brains are like sponges and the more we learn, the smarter we will be. Don't forget how lucky you are to have the opportunity to learn!

Do what your teacher tells you to do and do it willingly and happily.

40

Treat others the way you'd like to be treated

Remind yourself that other students are a lot like you. They have family and friends just like you. They have feelings just like you. They have fears just like you.

Treating others the way you would like to be treated is really easy. You know how you would like to be treated, right? Okay then, just treat others that way!

Would you like someone to cut you in line? No, then don't do it to someone else.

Would you like someone to share with you? Yes, then you should offer to share with others. Easy right?

Always treat others the way you would like to be treated.

41

Respect differences

Everyone is different and that is okay. No one is better than anyone else. We are all human beings and we all have different likes and dislikes.

It is okay if you don't agree with a friend. Have you ever heard the saying, "Agree to disagree"? It means that it is okay if you disagree with someone. For example, not everyone likes dogs. If everyone liked dogs, then there would be so many cats without homes.

Everyone is different and that is okay.

42

Always do your best

Always do your best in everything you do. If you are working on math, do your best. If you are eating your lunch, use your best manners. If you are being nice to a friend, be as nice as you can be. If you are playing basketball, play the best game of basketball that you can. If you are helping your parents set the table, set the entire table; don't just half set the table. If you are helping your teacher clean up, give it your all and do your best.

Always try your best. Do not be lazy just because you can. Laziness is not a good quality to have. Laziness will get you nowhere and I mean nowhere.

Always do your best and give it all you've got!

43

Right from wrong

Inside your heart, you know right from wrong. You can feel it. When you do the right thing, you feel good inside. When you do something wrong, it makes you feel bad inside. I believe that when you do the wrong thing, it is bad for your body and health. I believe that telling the truth is as good for you as eating your veggies.

Doing the wrong thing puts knots in your stomach. Doing the right thing makes you smile inside.

Listen to your heart and always do the right thing.

44

Be happy and smile

Did you know that happiness is a choice? You get to choose what mood you are in. If something makes you grumpy, stop for a minute and replace your thoughts with things that make you smile. Sometimes when things make me laugh I will write it down so I don't forget it. Then whenever I am sad or mad, I will pull out the list of things that made me laugh and I will replace my sad or mad thoughts with happy ones.

Also smiling for no reason can help change your mood. The next time you find yourself grumpy, smile for several minutes and you will feel your mood change.

Choose to smile and be happy!!!

45

Positive or
negative thinking

Ever since I was a baby, my mom has always asked me "Is that a positive or a negative?" If I get mad at my sister and say something I shouldn't, my mom will ask the question: "Is that a positive or a negative?" Try to ask yourself that question from time to time. Are the things you do and say positive or negative? Are the thoughts you are thinking positive or negative? When you think positive, you will bring more positive things into your life.

Ask yourself, "Is that a positive or a negative?"

46

Wash your hands

Wash your hands often to keep yourself and your school healthy. Colds and the flu are spread easily and germs can be found on everything you touch. You are supposed to wash your hands while singing the happy birthday song twice. Many people just do a quick rinse and that doesn't get the germs off. It takes about 20 seconds to sing the happy birthday song and that is the recommended amount of time you should take to wash your hands. Remember to wash the tops of your hands up to your wrists and in-between your fingers and under your fingernails. Try to remember not to touch your nose, mouth, or eyes because this is another way that infections are spread.

Wash your hands several times a day and especially before you eat and after you go to the bathroom. This is not a time to be lazy.

47

Talk about
your feelings

A lot of people hold in their feelings. One time a friend of mine was acting mad at me all day and I didn't know why. At the end of the day, she finally asked me why I didn't wave to her during the morning recess. I must not have been paying attention because I didn't see her wave to me. I wish she had talked about her feelings with me earlier in the day. I apologized and told her that I didn't see her wave.

Talking about your feelings will always make you feel better.

48

Help out at
the end of the day

At the end of the day look around your area and make sure everything is put away and that nothing is on the floor around your desk. Then if there is time, ask your teacher what you can do to help him or her.

Clean up and help your teacher at the end of the day.

49

Create your life

There are many people who believe that you can create and get what you want with your thoughts. Some scientists believe that creating your life with your thoughts is a proven science. Isn't that a great idea?! Here's how it works: The night before school, picture in your head how you want the next day to go. Do you want others to be nice to you? Do you want to do well in school? Picture in your head (with your thoughts) people being nice to you. And picture yourself doing well in school. Can you see yourself getting a 100 on your spelling test? Great! Have fun with this and watch it work.

Create your day and your life with your positive thoughts.

50

Breathe

There is a lot to learn in grade school and there may be times when you feel overwhelmed because there is so much you are trying to remember. If you get frustrated take a few deep breaths. Deep breathing will help you feel better and think more clearly. You can take a few deep breaths right at your desk by breathing in and out your nose. Feel your belly fill up like a balloon with each breath. Breathing can make you feel better and help you relax.

Learn to take a few deep breaths if you get frustrated, upset, or nervous.

There you have it! 50 fun and easy tips you can do today and every day. You can do it! If you follow these simple rules, you are guaranteed to have grade school success. You can use these tips throughout your life as well.

If you would like to email us, letting us know how these tips have helped you have grade school success, we would love to hear from you. Email us your stories at:

gradeschoolsuccess@findyourwaypublishing.com

We look forward to hearing from you!

About the Author

Marrae Kimball is an honor student and lives in Maine. She loves helping others. She enjoys animals of all kinds, especially cats. Marrae is a musician and plays the viola, piano, and electric guitar. She likes to travel and recently took a trip to Paris, France and Germany. Marrae also enjoys fishing, archery, sailing, rock climbing, camping, dancing, biking, roller-coasters, and spending time with friends and family.

Marrae had the idea for this book one day after her mom came home from substitute teaching. She wrote this simple book to help students, parents, and teachers have grade school success. Marrae enjoys writing, takes pride in her work, and is currently working on several book ideas.

Disclaimer

The purpose of this book is for entertainment purposes only. The author and Find Your Way Publishing, Inc. shall have neither liability nor responsibility to any person or entity with respect to any loss or damage caused, or alleged to have been caused, directly or indirectly, by the information contained in this book. If you do not wish to be bound by the above, you may return this book along with a copy of the receipt to the publisher for a full refund.

Guaranteed Success for Grade School

50 Easy Things You Can Do Today!

Quick Order Form

Fax orders: 207-514-0438. Please send this form with your order.

Telephone orders: 207-514-0575

Internet orders: www.findyourwaypublishing.com

Postal orders: Find Your Way Publishing, Inc.

PO Box 667

Norway, ME 04268

USA

Please include:

Name of book:

Quantity:

Your Name:

Address:

City:

State:

Zip:

Telephone:

Email address:

Guaranteed Success for Grade School

50 Easy Things You Can Do Today!

Quick Order Form

Fax orders: 207-514-0438. Please send this form with your order.

Telephone orders: 207-514-0575

Internet orders: www.findyourwaypublishing.com

Postal orders: Find Your Way Publishing, Inc.

PO Box 667

Norway, ME 04268

USA

Please include:

Name of book:

Quantity:

Your Name:

Address:

City:

State:

Zip:

Telephone:

Email address:

www.ingramcontent.com/pod-product-compliance
Lightning Source LLC
LaVergne TN
LVHW051647080426
835511LV00016B/2535